Papeterie Bleu

#MOMLIFE2
RETURN OF TODDZILLA
A SNARKY ADULT COLORING BOOK

Illustrated by Micaela

ISBN-13: 978-1530774975
ISBN-10: 1530774977

#MOMLIFE

It's 6:30 PM. By some miracle, one of your kids is asleep while the other is watching cartoons in a food coma. Quick! Here's your chance! Grab some markers, this coloring book, and run to the bathroom (don't forget the wine)! First, lock the door and enjoy the solitude of private urination. Second, gulp down that wine and enjoy the most relaxing five minutes of your day as you surrender to the quietness and creativity of coloring. Celebrate the humor and frustration that are the highs and lows of motherhood featured in the pages of this book.
**#MOMLIFE IS THE BEST LIFE!
HAPPY COLORING!**

CLEANING WITH KIDS is like brushing YOUR TEETH while eating BROWNIES

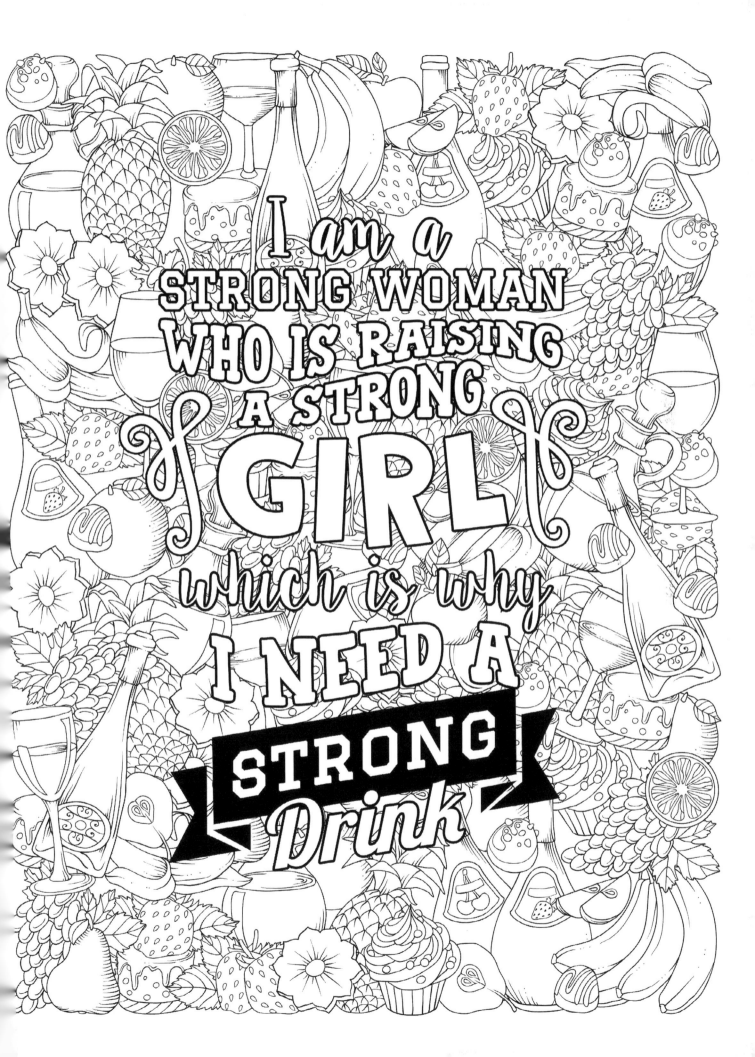

SORRY I RUINED YOUR LIFE BY ASKING you to put your shoes AWAY

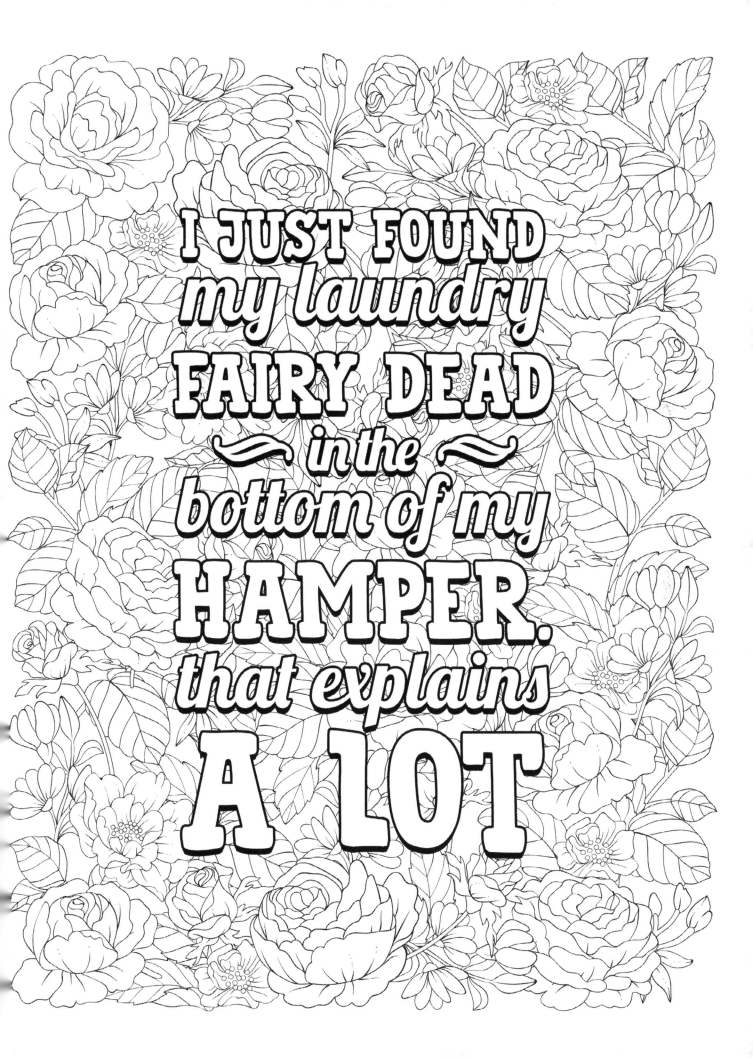

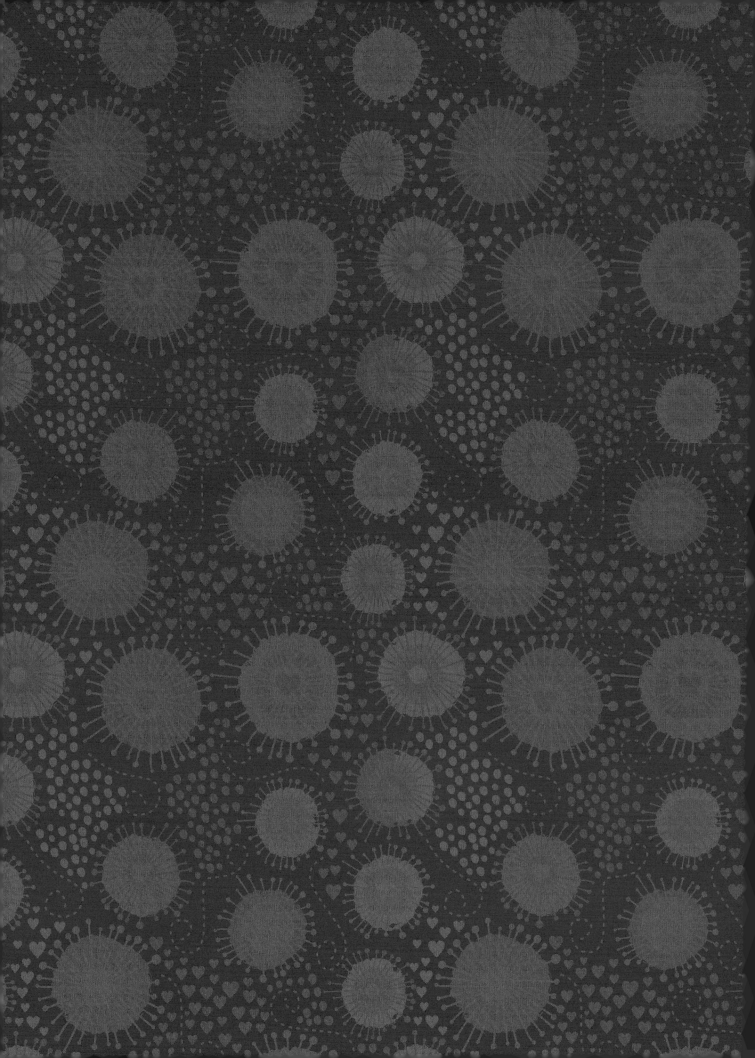

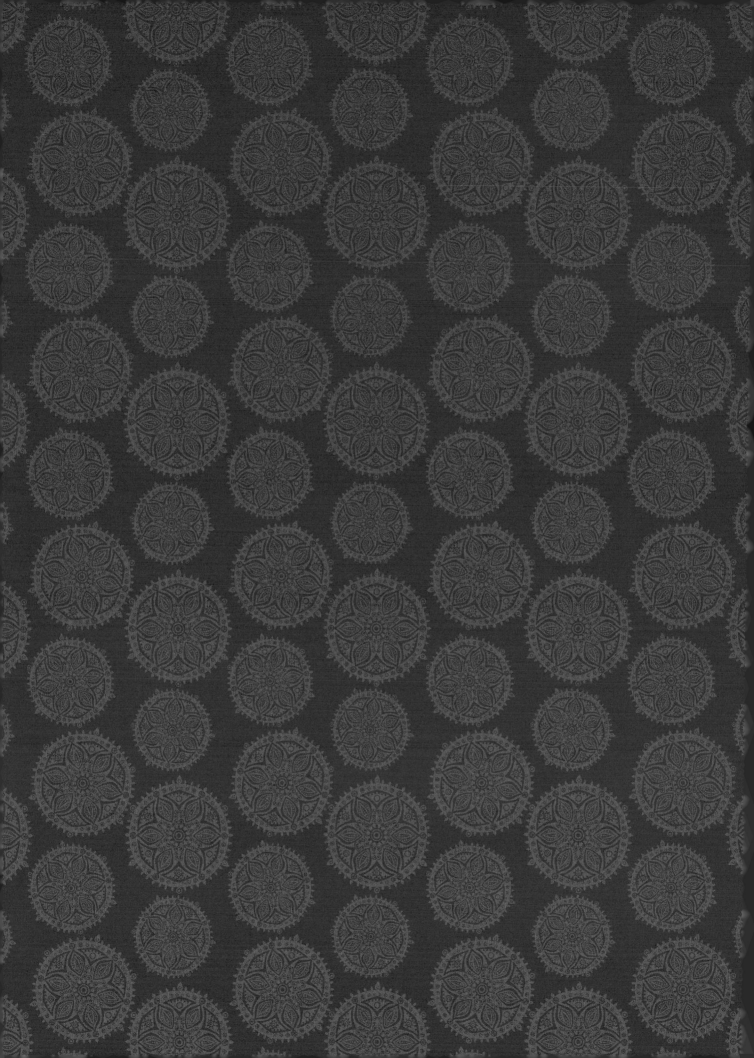

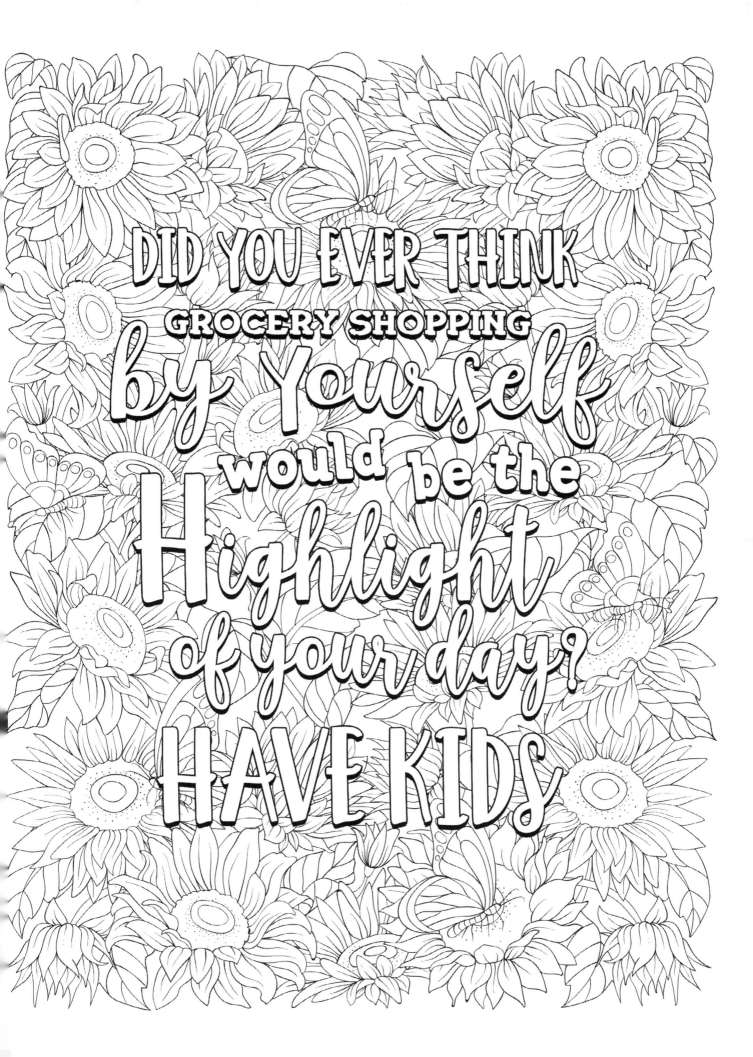

I JUST cleaned EVERYTHING from TOP to BOTTOM SO NOW I'M GONNA need EVERYONE to STOP living here

Get out!!

MOTHERHOOD IS : TELLING YOUR KIDS THEY can't eat cookies for BREAKFAST THEN EATING COOKIES FOR BREAKFAST AFTER they leave for SCHOOL

Someday your kids will be BIG enough to mow the LAWN and you will remember why you had them

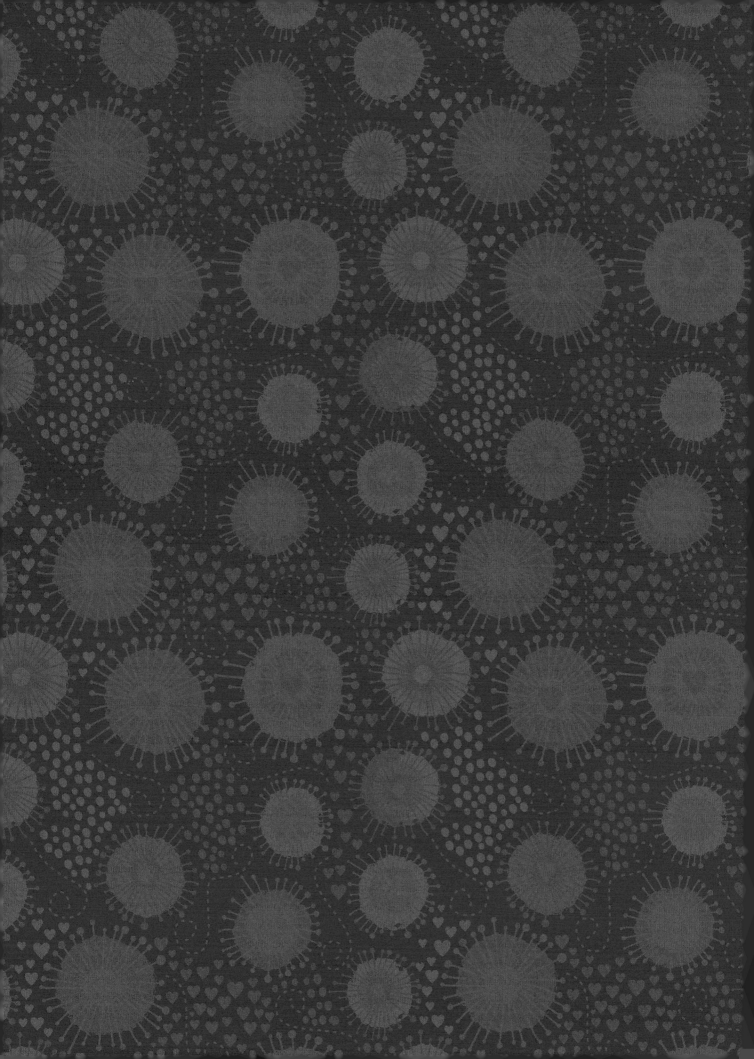

I HATE TO CANCEL.
I know WE MADE PLANS
TO GET
together tonight
but that was
2 HOURS AGO
I was
younger then,
AND FULL OF
HOPE

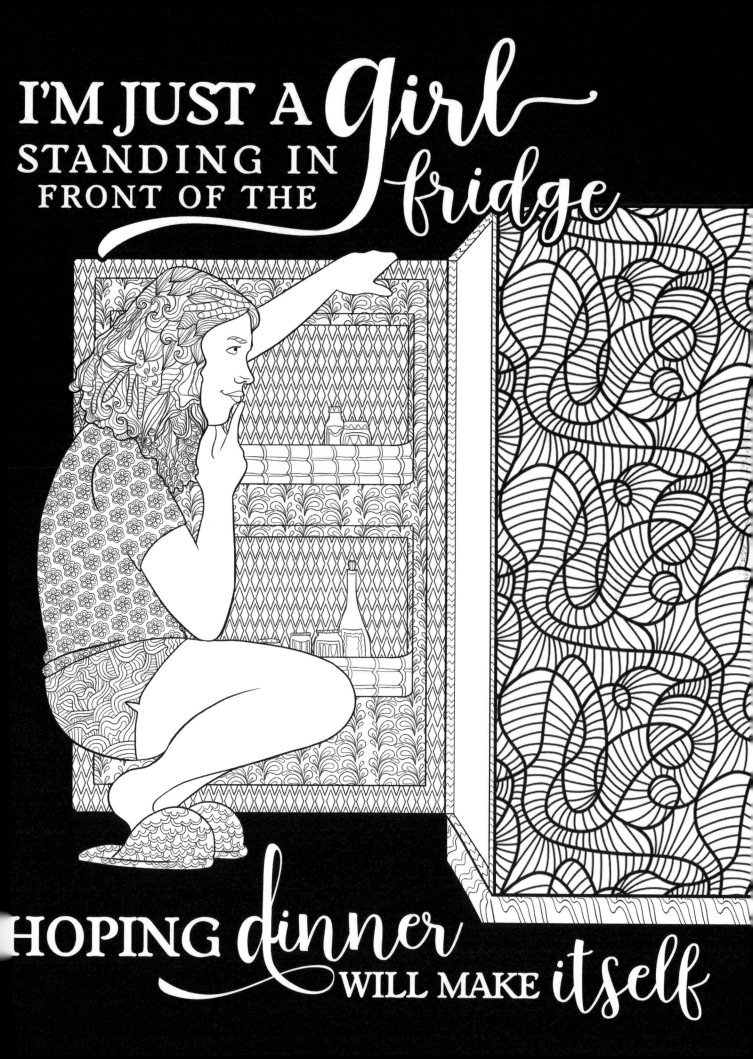

#STOPTHEMOMMYWARS

#ENDMOMMYWARS

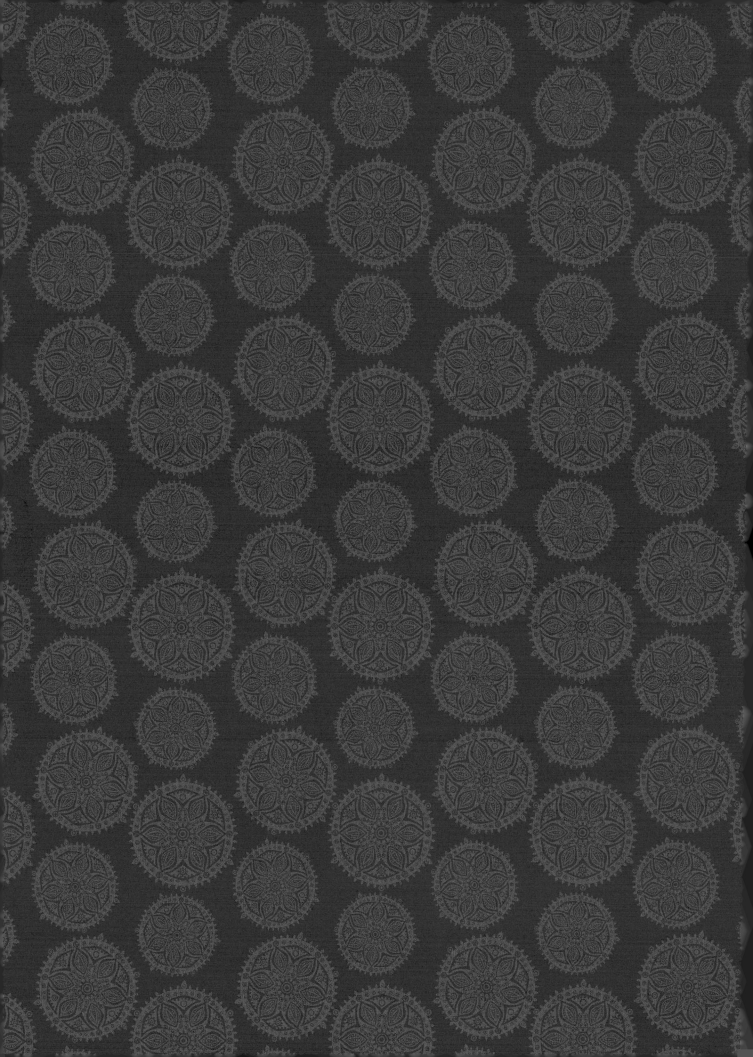

BE SURE TO FOLLOW US ON SOCIAL MEDIA FOR THE LATEST NEWS, SNEAK PEEKS, & GIVEAWAYS

@PapeterieBleu

Papeterie Bleu

@PapeterieBleu

ADD YOURSELF TO OUR MONTHLY NEWSLETTER FOR FREE DIGITAL DOWNLOADS AND DISCOUNT CODES

www.papeteriebleu.com/newsletter

FREE DOWNLOAD

www.papeteriebleu.com/momlife2

YOUR DOWNLOAD CODE: ML2756

@papeteriebleu

Papeterie Bleu

CHECK OUT OUR OTHER BOOKS!

www.papeteriebleu.com

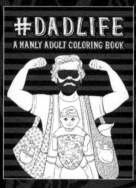

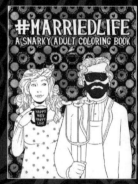

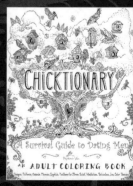

CHECK OUT OUR OTHER BOOKS!

www.papeteriebleu.com

CHECK OUT OUR OTHER BOOKS!

www.papeteriebleu.com

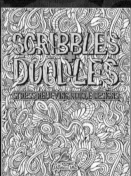

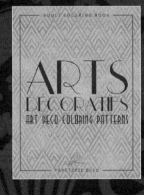

Made in the USA
Middletown, DE
11 May 2023

30371908R00046